TANG
HISTO

D0728388

JAPANESE AMERICAN INTERNMENT

Prisoners in Their Own Land

BY STEVEN OTFINOSKI

Consultant:
Richard Bell, PhD
Associate Professor of History
University of Maryland, College Park

CAPSTONE PRESS
a capstone imprint

Tangled History is published by Capstone Press,
1710 Roe Crest Drive, North Mankato, Minnesota 56003
www.capstonepub.com

Library of Congress Cataloging-in-Publication Data

Names: Otfinoski, Steven, author.
Title: Japanese American internment : prisoners in their own land / by
Steven Otfinoski. Description: North Mankato, Minnesota : Capstone Press,
[2020] | Series: Tangled history | Includes bibliographical references and
index. | Audience: Grades 4-6. | Audience: Ages 8-12. Identifiers: LCCN
2019007449| ISBN 9781543572575 (hardcover) | ISBN 9781543575576
(pbk.) | ISBN 9781543572612 (ebook pdf) Subjects: LCSH: Japanese
Americans—Evacuation and relocation, 1942-1945—Juvenile literature.
| World War, 1939-1945—Japanese Americans—Juvenile literature. |
Japanese—United States—History—Juvenile literature. Classification:
LCC D769.8.A6 O85 2020 | DDC 940.53/1773089956—dc23. LC record
available at https://lccn.loc.gov/2019007449

Editorial Credits
Michelle Bisson, editor; Kazuko Collins, designer; Eric Gohl, media
researcher; Laura Manthe, production specialist

Photo Credits
AP Photo: Jeff Chiu, 101, William P. Straeter, 100; Getty Images: Alex
Garcia, 104, Carl Mydans, 86, Carnegie Museum of Art/Teenie Harris
Archive, 94, George Rodger, 96, Leonard McCombe, 79, Mondadori
Portfolio, 92, The Denver Post, 81; Library of Congress: 7, 17, 29, 36, 39,
45, 56, 62, 65, 68, 84; National Archives and Records Administration: 4, 8,
15, 20, 25, 30, 42, 49, 52, 71, 75; Newscom: Everett Collection, cover, UIG
Universal Images Group/Underwood Archives, 11, ZUMA Press/Sara A.
Fajardo, 103; Wikimedia: Public Domain, 23, UNESCO, 98

All internet sites in the back matter were available and accurate when this
book was sent to press.

Printed and bound in the United States of America.
PA70

TABLE OF CONTENTS

More than 1,170 crewmen were killed when the Japanese attacked and sank the USS *Arizona*.

FOREWORD

The United States had managed to stay out of the world war that engulfed Europe in September 1939 with Germany's invasion of Poland. The U.S. had also resisted getting involved in Japan's aggression in Asia, where it had entered into a full-scale war against China in 1937. That changed on a sunny morning in early December 1941. That day, December 7, the Japanese launched a surprise attack on the U.S. naval base at Hawaii's Pearl Harbor. Some 2,403 Americans, including 68 civilians, were killed, six battleships were damaged, and two were destroyed.

The next day the United States declared war on Japan and three days later declared war on its Axis power partners, Germany and Italy. Many Americans felt they were in imminent danger of another attack. If the Japanese could destroy Pearl Harbor, what was to stop them from launching a follow-up attack on the West Coast of the United States? Suspicions turned to Japanese Americans, who made up 1 percent of the population of California, more than 93,000 people. Could they be aiding the enemy by spying, sabotaging American industry, or committing other treasonous acts? With not a shred of evidence of this, the U.S. government let fear drive it to act on its worst impulses.

The U.S. government immediately imposed restrictions on Japanese Americans. They ordered the closing of Japanese language schools. Japanese Americans on the West Coast owning shortwave radios and cameras had to turn them in to the government. Then on January 29, 1942, U.S. Attorney General Francis Biddle issued an order establishing "strategic military areas" on the Pacific coast. All suspected "enemy aliens" in these restricted areas had to observe curfews at night and would eventually be removed from these areas. In truth, two-thirds of all Japanese Americans in these areas were American-born citizens. These Japanese American citizens fell into one of two categories. Nisei were the children of parents who immigrated from Japan. Sansei were the grandchildren of Japanese immigrants. These parents and grandparents who came from Japan were known as Issei, and the majority of them were not naturalized U.S. citizens. Because they retained much of their Japanese traditions in terms of language and culture, they were the first to be suspected of aiding the enemy.

President Franklin Delano Roosevelt signed Executive Order 9066 on February 19. The order authorized the War Department to officially establish these "military areas" or zones from which any or all suspicious people would be removed.

Manzanar was the first of 10 internment camps for Japanese Americans.

By March 2 the First Zone was designated to include the western parts of California, Washington State, Oregon, and southern Arizona. Zone 2 included the remaining parts of these four states. Later that month, the first large group of Japanese Americans—including many families—were forced to leave their homes. They were sent to Manzanar War Relocation Center in eastern California. By September Manzanar housed more than 10,000 Japanese Americans. More than 110,000 other Japanese Americans were sent to nine other internment camps. This roundup of innocent people would become one of the darkest chapters in American history.

The attack on Pearl Harbor brought the United States into World War II and cast suspicion on blameless Japanese Americans.

EVACUATION

Eighteen-year-old Susumu Satow was playing catch with his father when the news came over the radio. The American naval base at Pearl Harbor in Hawaii had been bombed by the Japanese in a surprise attack.

Susumu, known as "Sus" to family and friends, couldn't believe it. As a Japanese American he felt terrible—both for his country and his family.

"What is going to happen to us?" he asked his father.

Mr. Satow shook his head, a troubled look on his face. "It is not going to be good," he said.

Sus wasn't sure what his father meant, but he knew that he was usually right.

Mine Okubo

Mine Okubo was eating a late breakfast in her kitchen when she heard the news on the radio. The Pearl Harbor attack was shocking, but she didn't think it would affect her or her brother much. Her brother, Toku, was a student at the University of California at Berkeley, where Okubo had received two fine arts degrees. Now age 29, Okubo was a professional artist working for the Federal Arts Project. For two years she had been creating mural projects for Fort Ord and the Servicemen's Hospitality House in nearby Oakland. She was proud to be an American and was using her creativity to give back to her country. No one could accuse her of being a Japanese sympathizer. What did she have to fear?

Isamu Noguchi

Isamu Noguchi sat back and enjoyed the warm California sunshine as he drove his car down the roadway. A well-known sculptor at age 37, he was heading to San Diego to look at some stone for

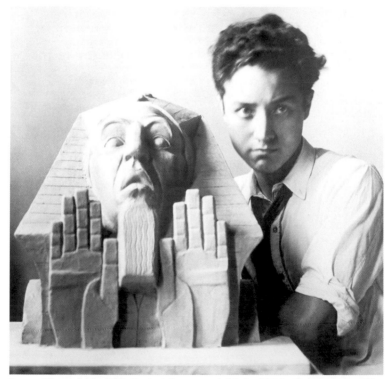

Isamu Noguchi had his first sculpture exhibit in 1924, when he was still a college student. This sculpture, *Paphnutius*, was part of the exhibit.

his sculpting. Noguchi had enjoyed his time in California but looked forward to returning to his home in New York City. Suddenly an announcer interrupted the music on his car radio. Hawaii's Pearl Harbor had been attacked by the Japanese, the announcer said. Noguchi was saddened and angered at the news. It hit close to home. His mother was white and born in the United States. His father was a famous Japanese poet. He lived in Tokyo and wrote propaganda for the imperial government of Japan. Noguchi felt he had to do something to make up for his father's support of America's enemy. He resolved to return to New York as soon as possible and see what he could do to help the United States in this new conflict with Japan.

Masao Itano

The jail at Sacramento
February 17, 1942, 2:00 p.m.

Masao Itano knew he had done nothing wrong. But with the hysteria in the country since the Pearl Harbor attack, that didn't seem to matter. The United States was now at war with Japan and its Axis partners in Europe, Germany, and Italy. Almost daily, it seemed more and more restrictions were put on Japanese Americans. Just a few weeks before, the attorney general had set up "strategic military areas" on the West Coast from which suspected aliens would be removed. Itano did not see himself as an alien. He had come to the U.S. at age 17 from Japan to go to college, start a new life, and raise a family. Nevertheless, the previous day Federal Bureau of Investigation (FBI) agents had come to his house and arrested him on suspicion of being "an enemy alien." It was all a terrible mistake, Itano thought. Then police officers told him they were transporting him to another jail but wouldn't tell him where.

As Itano was led out by the officers, a crowd stood watching. He felt nothing but shame at being seen in handcuffs like a common criminal. Then suddenly he spotted his wife, Sumako, in the crowd. She waved to him. But his only thoughts now were for his son, Harvey, who was soon to graduate from college. "Tell Harvey to continue to study," he yelled to her.

"I already did," she called back. And before he could say another word to his wife, the officers hustled him into a police car and drove off.

Susumu Satow

Sacramento, California
February 20, 1942, 2:30 p.m.

Sus's father was right when he said things would turn bad for them after Pearl Harbor. At school, classmates that Sus used to be friendly with now looked at him with cold stares. As he walked home from school he passed handwritten signs that read JAPS MUST GO. They were talking about him! An American! Why, he'd rather play baseball than go to Japanese language school! Only the day before, President Roosevelt had signed the order that singled out Japanese Americans living in what was now called a war zone.

As he arrived home from school, Sus was surprised to see several FBI agents in the house, going through the family's things.

"What are they doing?" he asked his father.

Japanese Americans protested the evacuation order with signs such as these, as shown in this photo by Dorothea Lange.

"They are looking for evidence of subversion," replied his father. "But they won't find any."

"Oh no?" said one of the agents, holding a large, leather-bound book in his hands. "What's this book? It's written in Japanese."

"That, sir," said his father, barely controlling his anger, "is our family Bible."

His mother, who looked pale, pointed to the painting of Jesus and his disciples at the Last Supper on the living room wall. "See?" she said. "We are good Christian people. Good Americans!"

The agent said nothing. He went into the next room where two other agents were looking through the family's things. "Okay," he said. "We're done here. Let's go."

When the agents had gone, Sus's mother hugged his father and cried. Sus looked around at the clothes scattered on his bedroom floor. He felt like their house had been defiled.

Isamu Noguchi

Washington, D.C.
March 31, 1942

"It's good to see you, Isamu," said Commissioner of Indian Affairs John Collier, welcoming his old friend to his office.

Noguchi explained he was ready to help with the war effort in any way he could. He complained that his offer had been turned down by every official in Washington, D.C.

"They're politicians," said Collier. "They don't know what to do with an artist like yourself. But I think I have an idea that you might like."

Collier explained how the internment camps being built would need personnel to work with the internees.

The buildings in which Japanese Americans were forced to live in Poston were quickly and poorly constructed.

Noguchi had heard about the internment camps. Putting Japanese Americans like himself in camps when there was no evidence that they were disloyal to the U.S. was wrong. But he listened politely as his friend continued.

"You could teach art and organize art projects for your people," said Collier. "You could help turn Poston into a model community."

"Poston?" said Noguchi.

"Poston, Arizona," explained Collier. "It's on Indian reservation land, which I oversee. I could make arrangements for you to go and live there. Of course, you'd be a volunteer and not under any restrictions as the other residents would be."

The idea appealed to Noguchi. He knew few other Japanese Americans in New York. He would be able to get to know the West Coast Nisei and help these people express themselves through art. There was just one thing he wanted to be clear about.

"You said my stay there would be strictly voluntary," he said.

"Of course," said the commissioner. "You would be free to leave at any time."

"Then I'll go," said Noguchi, already looking forward to this new adventure.

Dorothea Lange

Washington, D.C.
April 8, 1942, 12:30 p.m.

Photographer Dorothea Lange left the office of the War Relocation Authority (WRA) with a bounce in her step. She had just been hired to take pictures documenting the relocation program for Japanese Americans. Lange was already famous for her compelling photographs of migrant workers during the Great Depression (1929–1939). Now she was eager to document the Japanese Americans being sent to internment camps. She was determined to portray how these people were being unjustly rounded up and sent to the camps as honestly as she could. People were already on their way to temporary assembly centers while the internment camps were being built. Lange had started taking pictures weeks earlier but now would be on the payroll.

Families had little time to prepare to leave their homes and could take very little with them, as shown in this photo by Dorothea Lange.

Hiroshi Kashiwagi

Loomis, California
April 10, 1942

Hiroshi Kashiwagi awoke with a start on the living room floor. He'd slept there because their beds had all been stripped and put away. *This is the day,* he thought to himself. *This is the day we must leave our home.* He woke up his younger brother and sister, and told them to get dressed. His mother was already gathering their suitcases and duffle bags. Kashiwagi could smell the cooked chicken in the bags. The previous day he had killed the 18 chickens they owned. Then his mother had cooked them with soy sauce and sugar and put them in mason jars. That would be their main food until they arrived at the assembly center.

Kashiwagi wished their father was going with them. But he was sick with tuberculosis and had been taken to a nearby hospital. When he was better, his father would join them. Before being hospitalized, Kashiwagi's father had slept in a tent outdoors so he wouldn't infect other family members. Then Kashiwagi's mother had cut up the tent to make their duffle bags.

Kashiwagi had no sooner dressed than he heard the sound of a car horn outside. He looked out and saw the owner of the farm they worked on standing next to his pickup truck. The man handed the keys to Kashiwagi. He was loaning him the truck to drive to the departure point. Kashiwagi thanked him. Now they wouldn't have to walk the 3 miles (4.8 kilometers) to the departure place with their bags and suitcases.

Mine Okubo

Berkeley, California
May 1, 1942, 8:00 a.m.

Twenty-nine-year-old artist Mine Okubo had been wrong about not being targeted by the United States as an alien enemy. To the government she was not anyone special, just another Japanese American who had to be watched over. She and her brother weren't even people anymore. They were numbers. Several days earlier, she had gone to register at the Berkeley First Congregational

Mine Okubo had a promising career ahead of her when she was interned.

Church and had been given a "family number." It was 13660. As she and Toku were driven by friends to the bus station, she looked at the number pinned to her clothing. At the station they said their goodbyes and climbed onto the bus designated for the internees.

Sato Hashizume

Although she had been born in Japan while her mother was visiting family, 10-year-old Sato Hashizume had been raised in Portland. Her mother died when she was three and her father ran an apartment building. Now they were going to leave their home behind to go to an assembly center. They had to sell most of their possessions, but one thing they would not sell—her mother's piano. It was one of the few keepsakes Sato had left of her mother and she would not give it up.

Just then, a woman from the Young Women's Christian Association (YWCA) came and asked if there was anything she could do to help. Sato told her about the piano. "I'll take it for you," said the woman. "I'll keep it for you." Then she offered to drive them to the assembly center.

Sato was so relieved she gave the woman a hug.

University president Robert Sproul (center) soon came to regret his role in the internment of Japanese American students.

Robert Gordon Sproul

University of California, Berkeley
May 10, 1942, 1:00 p.m.

University president Robert Gordon Sproul was not a man to hide the truth. This made his position at the graduation ceremony all the more awkward.

As the moment for the presentation of student academic awards arrived, Sproul stepped up to the podium.

"I regret the recipient of the Gold Medal for Most Outstanding Student, Harvey Itano, could not be with us today," he said. "Harvey could not be here because his country called him elsewhere."

The sighs of disappointment gave way to loud applause among students and parents. They guessed that Itano had enlisted for the armed services. Only Sproul knew the ugly truth: Itano's "elsewhere" was not a battlefield but an assembly center. The government had conspired against this gifted young man, and Sproul had played his part in the conspiracy. The applause died down and the ceremony continued. Sproul vowed to himself that he would do whatever lay in his power to help Itano.

Marielle Tsukamoto

Florin, California
May 30, 1942, 8:00 a.m.

Five-year-old Marielle didn't understand what was happening. Why were they having to leave the home they loved, and so quickly? Worst of all, why did they have to leave one family member behind? Marielle loved her dog, but her mother said they didn't allow pets where they were going. The dog would have to stay behind and be cared for by a neighbor until they returned. As they prepared to leave, Marielle stroked her dog's head for the last time. She looked into its big brown eyes while tears fell from her own eyes.

Her mother gently pulled her away from the dog. "Here," she said and handed Marielle her favorite stuffed animal, a rabbit in blue velvet pants. "Come," she said. "It's time to go."

Marielle followed her parents and Granny out the back door of their home. Granny stopped by her roses in the garden and began to cry. Marielle forgot her own loss and took Granny's wrinkled hand in hers. "We will come back, Granny," she said softly. "Everything will be okay."

Susumu Satow

Sacramento, California
May 31, 1942

The train was waiting for the Satows when they arrived at the station. Sus and his family had been allowed only a week to pack and prepare to leave. The timing was bad. Sus was just a month from high school graduation and their crop of strawberries was nearly ready for harvesting. Mr. Satow got friends to promise to pick the strawberries after they were gone and sell them. The family had sold whatever things they had that they couldn't take with them. They sold their car, a Buick, for a mere $25. It seemed to Sus that people were taking advantage of their misfortune.

As they approached their train, Sus saw armed soldiers standing guard. It made him feel as if they were criminals. *Maybe this is just the beginning,* Sus thought. *They may very well send us to Japan. But why? We are Americans!*

Susumu Satow was just one of thousands of Japanese Americans leaving San Francisco for an internment camp.

TEMPORARY HOUSING

2

Japanese Americans lined up for inspection at Tanforan.

Mine Okubo

Tanforan Assembly Center,
San Bruno, California
May 1, 1942, 11:00 a.m.

The bus ride to Tanforan took about an hour, but it was a world away from the life Okubo had known at Berkeley. Tanforan was a race track, and the barracks where they would be living were actually horse stables. Upon arrival, Okubo and her brother were separated. They stood in separate lines of men and women for medical examinations and were told to undress. A nurse looked into Okubo's mouth with a flashlight and searched her body for vaccination marks. Then they were directed to an office desk where a woman would give them their room assignment.

"I'm sorry," said the woman, "but we will have to send you and your brother to separate quarters. We are short of rooms for small family units."

Okubo stared at the woman. "That is unacceptable," she replied. "My brother is the only family I have here and I will not allow you to separate us."

The woman argued with her until Okubo demanded to see her supervisor. The supervisor finally agreed to let them stay together.

Okubo and Toku crossed center field, a mess of mud and weeds, to their designated room. The walls of the stable room had been whitewashed but horsehairs stuck out between wall boards. The room reeked with the smell of horse manure. And the linoleum floor was covered with two inches of dust, which they cleaned with a whisk broom. The only furniture were spring cots they had to unfold. After dinner in the mess hall, they went to a stable where they were given bags of ticking to serve as mattresses and filled them with straw. Fortunately, Okubo had brought their own sheets and blankets.

By the time they got back to their room they were exhausted. They went to bed at ten o'clock that night, but the walls only rose part way to the ceiling and they could hear their neighbors. They heard a baby crying, a man snoring, and a couple whispering in the dark. Okubo, unable to sleep, stared up at the ceiling. She wondered how long they would have to stay in this place and what worse indignities lay ahead.

Marielle Tsukamoto

Fresno Assembly Center, California
June 1, 1942, 8:00 a.m.

Little Marielle awoke with a start on her army cot. There was an awful smell in the air. When she touched her head she felt something warm and sticky in her hair. She started to cry. Granny rushed to her side.

"It's all right, Marielle," she said. "You got that gooey stuff in your hair again. I'll wash it out."

The gooey stuff was tar from the tar paper on the roof of their barracks. This was the third time it had melted in the heat and dripped down on Marielle. The intense summer heat of Fresno in central California made life unbearable in other ways. When Marielle went out to play, sometimes her shoes would sink into the pavement's soft asphalt.

After several minutes of washing her hair, Granny stopped. "I'm sorry, dear," she said, "but the tar won't come out. We'll have to cut the sticky hair. It's the only way to get the tar off your head."

"Don't make me look bad, Granny," Marielle whimpered. "I don't want the other children to make fun of me."

"They won't, Marielle," said her granny soothingly. "I'll cut it so it looks like you just got a short haircut."

Marielle nodded and sat patiently as Granny clipped her hair with a pair of old scissors. When she finished, Granny held a small, cracked mirror up for her to see herself.

"It's okay," said Marielle. Then she left their tiny room with the rest of her family to go to breakfast in the mess hall. Marielle could feel the sweat dripping down her face as they walked. It was already very hot.

Isamu Noguchi

Poston, Arizona
June 4, 1942, 11:00 a.m.

Noguchi whistled a tune as he walked the empty streets of Poston. Weeks before, he had been one of the first people to arrive at the camp, and there were still only a few internees. As he walked, his head teemed with ideas for the future. He saw this as an opportunity to spread his love of art to the second-generation Nisei. Many of them had forgotten the handicrafts of their ancestral homeland. Besides conducting art classes, Noguchi wanted to set up craft guilds. Here, men and women could become skilled in ceramics, woodworking, and other traditional Japanese handicrafts. He couldn't wait to get started.

When he arrived at the mailroom he found a letter from his half-sister, Ailes. He read it and frowned. Ailes thought he had made a big mistake coming to Poston. The food, she wrote, would not be what he was used to and the heat would be unbearable. "I can only urge you to leave as soon as possible," she wrote. Noguchi smiled and shook his head. His sister meant well, but she didn't understand how important this was to him. Poston would give him a sense of purpose and fulfillment in this time of war. The heat and food were minor inconveniences. He would stay at the camp as long as he was useful. That was the commitment he had made and nothing would keep him from it.

Children at the North Portland Assembly Center could play on the swings and seesaws in the playground.

Sato Hashizume

Ten-year-old Sato should have been as unhappy as her elders. The North Portland Assembly Center, where they had lived since May, was an open arena with plywood stalls for living spaces, surrounded by a barbed-wire fence. Next door was a slaughterhouse that stank to high heaven. A cloud of flies from it migrated to the center. All six of Sato's family members lived in one crowded stall with a hanging cloth for a doorway. During the current heat wave the temperature reached 106 degrees Fahrenheit (41 degrees Celsius).

But despite all this, Sato saw life in the center as a continuous adventure. She spent most of her days outside. There was no school, so she was free to play with her old friends and make new ones. The adults didn't organize their playtime, so the children ran around, exploring every part of the center.

Sato recalled when they arrived there weeks earlier her father looked around and told her,

"Everything will be alright." And as far as Sato was concerned, it was just that.

Dorothea Lange

San Bruno, California
June 8, 1942, 4:30 p.m.

"Stop the car, Christina!" cried Dorothea Lange. Christina Page, her 22-year-old assistant, brought the old station wagon to a sudden halt. Lange, sitting on a platform atop the car, adjusted the lenses of her camera. Then she steadied the tripod it sat on. Along the roadside were families of Japanese Americans headed for the nearby Tanforan Assembly Center. She began taking picture after picture, quickly, before the people saw her. This was how she liked to work, photographing her subjects before they were aware of her presence. She wanted to capture them naturally, not posed for the camera or made self-conscious by it.

A boy looked up and saw her atop the car. He tugged on his mother's sleeve, and she and several other adults in their party looked up at her. Lange smiled and snapped a few more pictures. Then she called to her assistant to start moving again.

Dorothea Lange took thousands of photos of the internees with the large box camera in her arms. This photo of her became famous in its own right.

Lange sat down as the station wagon rumbled past the internees. It was still early, but Lange was exhausted. She had been photographing the internees at the assembly centers from morning to night for weeks. She traveled from her home in Berkeley to assembly centers in the California cities of Stockton, Salinas, and Sacramento. Now she was in San Bruno.

Everywhere she went she found it the same. The internees were living under the most squalid conditions. Nevertheless, they seemed optimistic and full of spirit. They reminded her of the determined migrant workers she had photographed years earlier during the Great Depression. She wondered what the authorities at WRA would think of her photos when they were processed back in Washington. If they expected them to reinforce the necessity of these camps, those authorities would be sorely disappointed.

"Let's head home, Christina!" she shouted down to her assistant.

"It's early yet," Page yelled out the car window. "And the Tanforan Center is just up the road."

Lange sighed. "Okay, you talked me into it," she replied. "Let's take a look around the center. Sleep can wait."

Bess K. Chin

Pomona Assembly Center, California
June 9, 1942, 7:30 p.m.

Eighteen-year-old Bess Chin didn't mind the poor conditions in Pomona or the fact that they were nine people living in one room. What she did mind was not having her mother there. After their arrival at the assembly center, Bess's mother got sick and went to the center's hospital. Every day Bess and her sister would visit their mother. The two girls lived in the room with her stepfather and his children. Bess herself wasn't in the best of health. She suffered from hypothyroid and as a result didn't have to work in the center. Having already graduated from high school, Bess didn't have to go to school either. She spent most of her days reading and thinking about the camp they would go to when they left Pomona. By then, she hoped, her mother would be better and they could be together again.

3

Harvey Itano had to spend only a few months in an internment camp.

WELCOME TO CAMP

Harvey Itano

Itano was reading a book on his bunk when he received a summons to the commander's office. Tule Lake, like each of the 10 internment camps, had a commander who ran it. The commander greeted Itano with an unfriendly stare. Harvey wondered whether he had done something wrong. If so, he wasn't aware of it.

"You have a visitor," said the commander. "He's in the next room."

The commander ushered him into the room and left without another word. To Itano's surprise the visitor sitting there smiling at him was President Sproul from the University of California, Berkeley. They shook hands warmly.

Sproul told Harvey he had good news for him. He'd been in touch with members of the National Japanese American Student Relocation Council and members of the government. Together, they had worked to get him released from Tule Lake. He would be sent to St. Louis University to continue his medical studies.

Itano was elated by the news, but one thought troubled him. "What about my family?" he asked.

President Sproul's expression turned more serious. "I'm afraid they will have to stay here for the time being," he said. "They are only allowing young people to leave right now."

Itano nodded. His parents would understand and be happy for him. "Be patient," said Sproul as he rose to leave. "It will only be a few more weeks. A member of the council will be in touch with you about your departure."

The commander asked Itano to stay behind. "I just want you to know, Itano, that I was against this decision," he said. "If it were up to me you would be staying here until this war is over. You and the rest of your kind."

Itano nodded and left. Nothing the commander could say could dampen his spirits. He ran back to his barracks to tell his mother the good news.

People at Manzanar waited in long lines to get into the mess hall for lunch.

John Tateishi

Manzanar, California
July 1, 1942, 11:25 a.m.

Three-year-old John Tateishi arrived on one of
the last trains of internees at the Manzanar station.
He had to stay behind when his family left weeks
earlier from the assembly center. He had come down

with German measles and so was quarantined at Los Angeles General Hospital. Many a night he cried himself to sleep in his lonely hospital bed. Now here at last he was reunited with his mother, who hugged him tightly. How good her arms felt! The camp barracks they lived in were bare looking, but John didn't care. He was with his family again and that was all that mattered.

In the afternoon, after they had lunch in the mess hall, his mother took him for a walk. They came to the barbed-wired fence that surrounded the camp. "Listen to me, son," she said, her face turning serious. "You are to stay at all times with your brothers when you are outside. And you are never, *ever* to go outside the fence. Do you understand?"

John nodded. Then he looked up at the armed guard standing atop the nearby tower. He didn't know what would happen to him if he did go outside the fence and was afraid to ask. He knew it had to be something bad.

Isamu Noguchi

Poston, Arizona
July 27, 1942, 2:00 p.m.

Noguchi sat slumped at his desk in the Arts and Handicrafts Center he had worked so hard to set up. All his work now seemed in vain. No one came to the center to take classes. The Nisei here had little interest in crafts or any of the arts. They were mostly working-class men, farmers, and laborers. They were good men, but had no intellectual curiosity. They were not even interested in the political situation that had placed them in the internment camp. He just didn't fit in with these people. They were mostly younger men with families, while he was single.

Too late, he realized his dream of finding solidarity with the Nisei was just that, a dream. Still, he thought if he could travel to other camps he might find people who would be interested in his mission. But his requests to leave were ignored or put off by the camp authorities. If he had come into Poston as a volunteer, he now was considered just another internee. He wrote Commissioner Collier, but he only put him off too. Now he was writing him again, expressing the desperateness of his situation.

"After much hesitation and with deep regret I must finally ask you to do what is necessary to have me released . . ." he wrote. "As you know I sought some place where I might fit into the fight for freedom. This might have been the place were I stronger or more adaptable. As it is I become embittered. I came here voluntarily, I trust that you will not have difficulty in securing this request.

"P.S. I might add it's the heat that drives me frantic."

Hiroshi Kashiwagi

Tule Lake, California
August 2, 1942, 1:30 p.m.

When it came to camp life, 20-year-old Hiroshi Kashiwagi of Loomis, California, could handle the hardship. It was the boredom that was driving him crazy. When he wasn't working in the mess hall, he spent his time reading and playing cards with friends. As for the camp itself, Tule had one thing that the assembly center didn't have—flush toilets. Other

Japanese Americans who were interned were each tagged with identifying numbers when they traveled to the camps, as shown in this photo by Dorothea Lange.

than that, the barracks, the dust, and the heat were depressingly similar.

He decided to take a walk around the camp and spotted a sign on the mess hall wall. It was posted by the recreation department. It asked anyone interested in starting a theater group in the camp to come to a meeting. Kashiwagi had no experience acting, but he loved plays and thought it would be fun to be in one. Besides that, working on a play would be something to fill up the empty hours. He decided he'd go to the meeting.

Dorothea Lange

San Francisco, California
August 5, 1942, 11:00 a.m.

Dorothea Lange waited nervously outside the office of Major Beasley. This wasn't the first time she had been called before Beasley, an army official in the War Relocation Authority. He was suspicious of her motives for photographing the internment camps. He felt she was doing more harm than good for the program. "Bozo" Beasley, as those who thought him not fit for his job called him, had bothered her before about reimbursement for her mileage and gas receipts. She was also certain that he encouraged military police at the camps to try to prevent her from talking directly to internees. What he was after her for now she didn't know.

"The major will see you now," said a young secretary.

Beasley wasted no time once she entered the office. "What's the meaning of this?" he cried, slapping a pamphlet down on his desk.

The pamphlet, which denounced the internment, featured one of her photographs on its cover. She remembered giving the photo to her friend who created the pamphlet.

"It's my photo," she admitted.

"Exactly," said Beasley. "I think this pamphlet is grounds for your dismissal from the program, Miss Lange."

"Wait a minute, Major," she said. "Whether you know it or not, that photo was first published by a congressional investigative committee. And that means it is in the public domain. Anyone could use it."

Beasley looked perplexed. "I'll check on that," he grumbled.

"You do that, Major," she replied. "Now may I go?"

"Of course," said Beasley. "But know that I'm watching you, Lange. Your job is to document the camps, not to take photos that are critical of the government. Understand?"

"Perfectly," she replied and left. For her, documenting and criticizing were one and the same thing.

Many young Japanese Americans spent their early years in camps. This was one of many photos of the camps taken by Dorothea Lange.

Sato Hashizume

En route to Minidoka, Idaho
September 15, 1942, 7:00 a.m.

All day and night young Sato and her family rode the train across Oregon. She watched the sun as it set over the desert when they entered Idaho and imagined what a wonderful place their new home away from home would be. As night turned to morning, she sang a new song, "Beyond the Hills of Idaho," with the other girls in her car.

Soon they arrived at the Minidoka train station, where buses and army convoy trucks were waiting to take them to the camp. To Sato's disappointment, it was no paradise in the desert. Minidoka looked like an army camp, with six barracks on either side of a mess hall. The barracks were bare, with no insulation and only six cots and a pot-bellied stove for furnishings.

"Where will we sit?" Sato asked her father.

"Don't worry," he said. "I will build us a bench out of wood. And some boxes to store things in. We will make this into a home."

Suddenly the permanence of their situation began to sink it. Sato's sense of adventure was beginning to fade. She asked her father how long it would be their home. He said he wasn't sure, but she shouldn't worry about it.

But Sato did worry. She was starting to miss her real home. When would she see it again?

Mine Okubo

Topaz, Utah
September 18, 1942, 8:00 a.m.

It had been a long and dreary train ride for Okubo and her brother from Tanforan Center to the deserts of Utah. The cars were old and dirty. Children cried during the night. People got sick on the train and vomited. The blinds were kept shut so they couldn't see where they were going. Or perhaps so people in the stations they passed through couldn't see them—Japanese Americans going to an internment camp.

Now they had finally arrived at their destination. A man boarded the train to welcome them to Topaz. He handed out copies of the *Topaz Times,* a camp publication that gave information for newcomers. Then they left the train and climbed into a waiting army convoy truck for the 17-mile (27.4-km) ride to the camp. Okubo didn't expect it to be much better than the assembly center and she wasn't wrong. The barracks were covered with tar paper. A strong wind and the soft alkali dirt make every step a struggle.

She and her brother, Toku, were sent to Block 7, Barrack 11, Room F. The large rectangular room was bare but for a ceiling light and a closet by the door. A thick layer of alkali dust blanketed the floor.

"Time to get out the whisk broom again," she said.

Toku laughed. She laughed too. Better to laugh than cry, she thought.

Crews worked on electrical wire in the camps.

4

LIFE BEHIND THE BARBED WIRE

Sato Hashizume

Minidoka, Idaho
September 21, 1942, 9:30 a.m.

Sato stepped into the dusty main street and waved her flag. The cars driving by came to a stop, and she ushered the younger schoolchildren across the street. Sato was proud of being a volunteer school guard for the two camp grade schools. It gave her a purpose, a sense of doing something useful. The job was not difficult. Almost the only vehicles that came rumbling down the road were military cars and trucks. Japanese American internees were not allowed to drive or own cars, and there were no bikes for the children in the camp. With no playground for them, about the only fun activity they could participate in was softball.

Sato was glad it wasn't raining. On rainy days the roads became pools of mud and the authorities put down planks to walk on. Without them, your shoes and feet would be sucked into the mud, making walking difficult.

Sato's thoughts were interrupted by a large bus that came rumbling down the road. Passengers in the bus looked out the windows and smiled and waved to her. Buses were rare in the camp, and she wondered where these happy people were going. She was sure it was a place with no dust and mud, a place where people could go about their lives freely. She wished she were on that bus going somewhere, anywhere, far away from Minidoka.

Hiroshi Kashiwagi

Tule Lake, California
September 25, 1942, 9:30 p.m.

Hiroshi Kashiwagi followed the other actors onto the stage for the final curtain call. He smiled and bowed as the audience applauded enthusiastically. It was their final performance of three one-act plays. In less than two months, the little theater group had come a long way from its first performance, a short skit performed outdoors. Now they were putting on plays on a makeshift stage in the mess hall. And the camp internees flocked to see them.

Kashiwagi discovered that he loved acting. The opportunity to play a character other than himself was great fun. He could forget about the situation he found himself in and lose himself in each role. He imagined the internees in the audience felt much the same. They could enter the world of each play and forget about the grimness of camp for a short time.

Kashiwagi was also discovering a love of writing. A writers' group formed soon after the theater group and Kashiwagi was one of the first to join it. He wrote stories, some of them about life in the camp. Getting out his thoughts and feelings on the written page was something he found extremely liberating. Between putting on plays, writing stories, and working in the mess hall, Kashiwagi was finding his life busier than ever. It was something he couldn't have imagined only a few short months ago.

Marielle Tsukamoto

Jerome, Arkansas
October 2, 1942, 5:00 p.m.

Marielle ran through the tall grass, chasing her friends in a game of tag. They were careful to steer clear of the swamp just beyond the grass. Her mother had warned her that rattlesnakes, water moccasins, and other venomous snakes lived in the swamp. Rural Arkansas was a world away from the home she knew back in California. But Marielle, for the most part, was enjoying this new world. The Jerome camp was a definite improvement over the assembly center back in California. It had a school, where she attended kindergarten. It had real bathrooms with flush toilets. The bad part was that the toilets had no dividers between them, offering no privacy. Marielle's Granny would stand in front of her when she sat on the toilet so other people couldn't see her.

Another good thing about Jerome was the fresh fruit and vegetables they got to eat. Men and women who were farmers were allowed to grow their own crops to feed the camp. They had no cows, but there were plenty of goats. Marielle got to like the taste of goat's milk. It was sweeter than the cow's milk she had been used to.

"You're it!" she cried, as she tagged one of her playmates. Just then they heard the loud clang of the dinner bell.

"Time to eat," said Marielle to her companions. "We'd better get back."

Dinner in the mess hall was only served for a short time. If you didn't get there in time, you missed a meal and went hungry. And after an afternoon of playing, Marielle was starving.

Bess K. Chin

Heart Mountain, Wyoming
October 10, 1942, 5:30 p.m.

Bess Chin looked over her limited wardrobe and picked out her one decent dress. She would wear it for her first night out of the camp since her arrival. Her life had changed since then in ways she could not have imagined. She had become a teacher's aide in an eighth grade English class and found she enjoyed teaching. The teacher she worked with was a kind and friendly young Caucasian woman. The woman's future father-in-law was the director of the camp hospital. He had invited Chin to join them for dinner that evening, a rare treat.

Chin was glad to make new friends. Her mother was back from the hospital, living with her and her

At camp socials, young internees could forget their cares and enjoy dancing.

younger sister. They had their own room at Heart
Mountain, separate from her stepfather. He was all
right, but Chin was happy to have their own place
with more room. Her older sister had married and
moved to Japan before the attack on Pearl Harbor.
Her brother lived in Minnesota, far outside the
war zone. He taught at a military intelligence
school there.

Chin wasn't as lonely as she'd been at the
assembly center. She learned how to crochet and
dance the jitterbug at the camp socials. She had even

learned to use some simple tools and had built a bench and a bookshelf for their room.

Just then her thoughts were interrupted by the honk of a car horn and she knew her ride was outside. She looked at herself one last time in a small mirror nailed to the wall. She looked presentable, she decided. Even pretty. She said goodbye to her mother and headed out the door for her big evening out.

Mine Okubo

Topaz, Utah
October 13, 1942, 11:00 a.m.

Okubo looked up at the white flakes softly drifting down from the ice blue sky. As with many of the internees, she had never seen snow before and found it a beautiful sight. Children were running around catching snowflakes in their hands and in their open mouths. Older children and some adults were making snowballs and hurling them at each other. It was a playful scene that Okubo decided was worth capturing. She grabbed the sketchpad out of her handbag and started drawing. She had been sketching scenes of camp ever since she had arrived at the Tanforan Assembly Center. Internees weren't allowed to have cameras, so she recorded what she saw in pen and ink or charcoal and sometimes even in watercolors. Someday maybe she would get them published. Her other creative outlet was writing with her brother for the *Topaz Times,* the camp newspaper. Okubo also taught art at the camp school, as she had back at Tanforan. The school at Topaz was better. It had more books and teaching materials and hired more internees to teach along with the Caucasian teachers. The white teachers were paid better, which bothered Okubo. It was just one more of the injustices they had to bear in the camp.

Susumu Satow

A sugar beet farm somewhere in Colorado
October 25, 1942, 5:00 p.m.

Sus took off his sweaty work clothes and headed for the showers. It was the end of another long day of harvesting sugar beets in the fields. He enjoyed the physical labor and the good feeling of tiredness that came with it. As soon as the authorities at the Poston camp asked for volunteers to do seasonal

Many of those interned were also used as unpaid agricultural workers.

work in neighboring Colorado, he applied. The camp offered few opportunities for work. He enjoyed playing baseball with the other boys but it wasn't enough to keep him busy. Working on the farm, he could almost imagine himself free of the camp and its restrictions. But in a few days the harvest would come to an end and he'd be back in Poston. He looked forward to seeing his family again but little else. He knew that if another opportunity arose to work outside the camp, he would take it.

Isamu Noguchi

It had finally come. After seven months in the camp, Noguchi was about to be released. In that time he had faced a string of disappointments. Not only had his arts center failed, but park and recreation areas he had planned were never built. He had designed blueprints for a school, a community center, a church, botanical gardens, and even a miniature golf course. The War Relocation Authority refused to allocate money for the labor and materials to build any of them. They rejected his idea of having the internees do the work themselves.

Now he had been given permission to leave the camp on a "temporary basis." But Noguchi had no intention of ever returning to Poston or any other internment camp. He saw no role for him there as an artist. He felt only pity for those Japanese Americans, who, unlike him, could not leave.

Driving his car through the main gate, he headed east for New York City. He planned to make only one major stop on the way. He wanted to visit his friend, architect Frank Lloyd Wright, in Wisconsin. Before leaving, he wrote to his sister, Ailes, telling her to let his friends in New York "know that I am on my way. I feel like Rip Van Winkle." Noguchi was comparing himself to the character in a classic American story who falls asleep for 20 years. He hadn't been away from home for that long, but it felt like it.

Winter in Manzanar was desolate.

SURVIVAL

Mr. Tateishi

Manzanar, California
December 1, 1942, 2:15 p.m.

Mr. Tateishi listened carefully to the words of his friend, Harry Ueno. Ueno was the head cook at the camp mess hall. He had noticed a shortage in their supplies of flour, sugar, and certain meats. "It's the guards or maybe the administrators who are stealing these supplies," Ueno said. "They are the only ones who have access to them. I tell you they are selling the food on the black market."

"What are you going to do about it?" asked Tateishi.

"I'm going to tell the camp commander," he said. "Then it will be up to him to do something about it."

"And what if he doesn't?"

Ueno's face turned red. "He'll have to," he said. "This is wrong. It's bad enough that they have taken away our freedom. Now they are taking the food out of our mouths!"

Tateishi shared his friend's anger. As one segment of Nisei known as Kibei, they were born in the United States but had spent time in school in Japan. Because of this they were well educated and knew their rights. Many Nisei had only lived in the United States and had never been part of an ethnic majority. They might be afraid to speak up, but not the Kibei.

"I will go with you," said Tateishi.

"No," said Ueno. "I don't want to get you in trouble too if anything goes wrong. It is more important that you organize our people to protest this wrong if they don't listen to me."

Tateishi reluctantly agreed. But he worried what would happen to his friend. And he also worried that other Nisei in the camp would be opposed to any protests against the authorities. The divisions between the two groups in the camp seemed to him at times wide. As wide as the divisions between the Japanese and the Americans.

Dorothea Lange

Berkeley, California
December 4, 1942, 11:00 a.m.

Lange looked at the photograph she'd taken, appearing in the latest issue of *Victory* magazine. It

Dorothea Lange's photos captured the humanity of those interned.

showed an elderly Japanese American man sitting
on a bed in a tiny room with partitioned walls. A
younger woman sits on the other end of the bed
and a light bulb dangles on a wire from the ceiling.
The picture showed just how cramped and stark the
living conditions were in Manzanar. But the caption
under the picture made no reference to this. Lange's

own detailed caption had been dropped. She tossed the magazine into a wastebasket in disgust.

Nearly all of her other photographs had been locked away by the War Relocation Authority, many with the word "IMPOUNDED" scrawled across them. Her work for the agency had ended. Lange was sure Major Beasley and other government officials were happy to be rid of her. She continued to work for the Office of War Information, but she no longer had access to the camps. She had wanted to make a difference with her photos. She had wanted to expose the evil of the camps to the American public. Now she wondered if her photos would ever see the light of day.

John Tateishi

Manzanar, California
December 6, 1942, 6:30 p.m.

John was worried. His father had left to go to the commander's office several hours ago and had not returned. He knew it had something to do with Mr. Ueno, who had been arrested the day before.

When he asked his father why this had happened, his father smiled sadly. "Because he spoke the truth," he said. That's when Mr. Tateishi left to see the commander.

After dinner, John sneaked off and started looking for his father. He was drawn to a crowd of internees standing in front of a building. As John watched, a door opened and out came his father and Mr. Ueno being led by guards. Their hands were handcuffed and there were shackles on their legs. John cried out but his father didn't hear him over the noise of the crowd. The guards pushed the two men into the back seat of a car. John watched as it drove off.

John spent the next few hours searching the camp for his father. He had to hide from the searchlights that circled the camp grounds. He had to dodge around the crowd of angry men running through the camp. At one point he heard the sound of gunshots and decided it wasn't safe. He ran back to the barracks. He said nothing to his mother or anyone else and went to bed. His sleep was interrupted by the angry shouts and running footsteps of men outside. *Would this terrible night ever end?* he thought. If they could arrest a good man like his father he didn't think any of them were safe.

Susumu Satow

Poston, Arizona
February 5, 1943, 2:00 p.m.

Sus was both elated and troubled. He was happy for himself but didn't know how his parents would take the news. Only a week earlier, President Roosevelt had announced that Japanese Americans could volunteer for combat duty in the U.S. armed services. All internees older than 17 had been given a questionnaire to fill out. It required them to declare their full loyalty to the United States. Sus had filled out the form and was now ready to enlist.

He entered the bedroom where his mother was resting after lunch to tell her his news.

His mother took it surprisingly well. She was proud that he would serve his country but worried about the dangers of the battlefield.

More than 30,000 Japanese Americans served in the U.S. military during and just after World War II.

He reassured her that he could take care of himself. He reminded her that he'd taken care of himself when he went away from Poston to pick sugar beets in Colorado. But this time he would be going far, far away. When he would return was anyone's guess. He wouldn't think about that now. He'd let his mother do the worrying for them both.

Hiroshi Kashiwagi

Tule Lake, California
February 10, 1943, 10:30 a.m.

Hiroshi Kashiwagi stared at the form on the table and read questions 27 and 28 for the third time.

"Are you willing to serve in the armed forces of the United States on combat duty, wherever ordered?

"Will you swear unqualified allegiance to the United States of America and forswear any form of allegiance or obedience to the Japanese Emperor or any other foreign power or organization?"

There was no doubt about it, the questions were an insult. Why should Kashiwagi want to serve the country that was holding him as a prisoner and enemy? And why should he have to pledge his loyalty? Like most of the young men in the camp, he had been born and raised in the United States. He was as American as anyone else. Why should the government question his loyalty to his country when he had done nothing wrong? However, if he were to answer "no" or refuse to answer these two questions, what would happen to him? Would he be thrown into prison like the two men at Manzanar had been for complaining about injustices there? Or even shot like the poor man who was part of the riot to protest the two men's arrest? He decided to ask his father for advice.

His father told him he and the other men in their family would answer "no" to questions 27 and 28.

Hiroshi was pleased to hear his father confirm his own thoughts. But he was also troubled.

"What will they do to us?" he asked.

His father put his hand on his son's shoulder. "Whatever they do it can't be any worse than what they have already done to us."

Sato Hashizume

Salt Lake City, Utah
March 5, 1943, 9:00 a.m.

Sato finished vacuuming the floors and immediately left the house of the woman she cleaned for. She didn't want to be late for school.

Her life had become busier than ever since her father came back to take her and her siblings out of the camp at Minidoka. Her father had tried to find work back in Portland but couldn't. Friends in Salt Lake City told him he could find work there. At first, Sato was happy to leave the camp behind, but freedom had its challenges too. Her father had been promised a job at a dry cleaner's in Salt Lake City. But when he arrived the job was given to someone else. Then he got a job as a cook in a restaurant. But the boss found out he didn't know how to cook eggs and demoted him to dishwasher. Then things got worse. While trying to catch his bus to work, her father slipped on ice and broke his pelvis. He was confined to bed for six weeks. To bring in income for the family, Sato went to work cleaning houses part-time. Her brother dropped out of high school to work in a produce market. Life was hard, but at least they were together. As she arrived at her first class in school, Sato wondered when she would make some friends. She knew no one in Salt Lake City. She longed to be back in Portland and wondered if she would ever see her home again.

Some Japanese Americans were able to get jobs in fruit markets after they were released from internment.

Harvey Itano

St. Louis, Missouri
April 8, 1943, 3:45 p.m.

Itano fingered the envelope nervously in his hands. Something was preventing him from opening it. It had been nine months since he left Tule Lake and came to St. Louis to attend medical school. He had done well in that time, excelling in all his classes. Like many of his classmates, he had applied for the Army's Specialized Training Program. Those students accepted would complete their medical training and then serve in the army overseas. Itano's application was turned down because he was classified as 4-C. This was the category for aliens and nationals with dual citizenship. But Itano fit neither category—he was a U.S. citizen! Determined, he applied again. Now the letter concerning his application had arrived. Reluctantly, he opened it. The good news was that he had been reclassified as 1-A for the draft. The bad news was that he was again rejected for the training program. Sadly, Itano realized that he hadn't left racism and prejudice behind when he left Tule Lake. He might be a medical student with a bright future, but many Americans only saw him as an untrustworthy alien.

Heart Mountain would lie empty for years after the internees were released.

Bess K. Chin

Heart Mountain, Wyoming
May 15, 1943, noon

Chin finished packing her suitcase. In another hour she would be on a train heading for Billings, Montana. From there she would continue on until she reached her final destination, St. Louis,

Missouri, where a new life awaited her. It was all thanks to a woman she knew years earlier when living in Japan. Her friend had since moved to St. Louis and invited her to join her there. The War Relocation Authority allowed Chin to leave because she had a job and a place to live. The job was as a technician at a medical school. It would pay for her tuition at St. Louis's Washington University. The only bad part was that her mother and sister would have to stay behind. And saying goodbye to them was a moment she dreaded.

Her mother stood by the door as she emerged from the bedroom with her suitcase.

"Take care of yourself and remember to eat well," her mother said, fighting back tears.

"We'll miss you," said her sister.

"I'll come back to visit," said Chin. Then she quickly added, "Of course, you'll be out of here soon and can come join me in St. Louis."

"I don't know," said her mother. "I think it'd be too cold for me. I want to go back to California. And you'll come back too."

"Of course, Mama," said Chin, wondering if she ever would go back. The war had so upset their lives that it was hard to tell what the future held. She could only hope that she really would see her family again soon.

6

The motto of the 442nd Regiment was "Go for Broke," meaning they would do anything to help win the war.

GOING HOME

Susumu Satow

Fort Douglas, Utah
July 29, 1943, 1:15 p.m.

Sus Satow stood tall and proud as the army officer inducted him into the all-Nisei 442nd Regiment Combat Team. He and the other Nisei volunteers weren't sure where they would be sent to serve, but knew that they would do their best wherever it was. Satow wished his mother and other family members could be there to see his induction. Yet he felt that, because young men like him were showing their patriotism, these dark days of internment would pass. One day soon, Japanese Americans would be accepted as equals by other Americans. In the meantime, there was a war to win.

The "no-no boys" were imprisoned in Tule Lake, California.

Hiroshi Kashiwagi

Tule Lake, California
October 8, 1943, 4:02 p.m.

Kashiwagi looked through the barbed wire fence as busload after busload of internees got off and entered the camp. The new fence was 8 feet (2.4 m) high. It signified the drastic changes that had taken place at Tule Lake. Where previously it had been an internment camp, now it was little more than a prison for supposed malcontents and troublemakers. The regular internees, the ones who had answered "yes" to questions 27 and 28 on the questionnaire, had been sent away to other camps. All those who refused to answer or answered no to these two questions were now being funneled into Tule Lake from other camps. It was becoming the largest camp of all.

They had a name for Kashiwagi and the other "disloyal" internees. They were called "no-no boys." It was meant to be a degrading term, but Kashiwagi took a certain pride in it. He was saying "no" not only to the loyalty act, but to all the injustices that his people had endured after the attack on Pearl Harbor. The authorities had pressured the no-no boys to renounce their U.S. citizenship. Kashiwagi had agreed to do that but was already wondering if he had gone too far in his protest in agreeing to do so.

The harsh voice of a guard came screeching through a bullhorn. "Stand back from the fence! Get away from the fence!" Kashiwagi did as he was told. But as he continued to watch the flood of new arrivals, an idea for a story came into his head. He couldn't wait to get back to his room to write it down.

Mine Okubo

Topaz, Utah
January 11, 1944, 10:45 a.m.

It was a long and busy morning for Okubo. She had to bring back her personal items to the block manager's office. Then she was off to gather the required signatures at the administration office on various forms. Here she would get her $25 train ticket that would take her all the way from Utah to New York City. A job awaited her there. Editors at *Fortune* magazine had seen her work and had offered her a full-time position as an illustrator. Her first assignment was to work on an issue about Japan. The War Relocation Authority had agreed to release her. Her brother had been allowed to leave seven months earlier.

Her suitcase in hand, Okubo moved toward the gate. A group of people had gathered to see her off. They were the very old and the very young. Everyone else had left. As she waved to them, she felt a lump in her throat but was determined not to cry. She climbed onto the bus that would take her to the train station and took a seat. She began to read a booklet that someone in the office had given her. It was titled, "When You Leave the Relocation Center." The bus pulled out and she read for a few minutes. Then she closed the booklet and shut her eyes. In that moment, her thoughts shifted from the past and present to a far brighter future.

Marielle Tsukamoto

Kalamazoo, Michigan
February 7, 1944, 9:30 a.m.

Marielle nervously mounted the front steps of her new school. She and her mother had left the camp at Jerome, Arkansas, months before. They joined her father and other relatives in Kalamazoo. A group of Methodists there had offered to sponsor them and that's why they were here. These good people had helped them find a place to live and jobs at a bakery for her father and uncle. They both worked the bakery's night shift and slept during the day. Marielle barely saw them. But, as her mother kept telling her, they had to adjust to their new life.

Entering her classroom, the other children stared at Marielle. Her teacher, who had a gentle voice, introduced her to the class. Though she was kind, the students were not. They teased Marielle during class. They poked and pinched her until she wanted to run out of the room crying. When the school day finally ended, she ran all the way home.

"They hate me," she said to her mother. "I don't want to go back there."

She expected her mother to say she had to, but she didn't. "You don't have to go back," she said softly. "Not for a while."

"Will it get better for us, Mama?" Marielle asked.

"I hope so, dear," she replied. "I really do."

Sato Hashizume

Portland, Oregon
March 25, 1944, 2:15 p.m.

Sato was finally back in Oregon. Her father, as always, was the first to return. He gave up his dishwashing job in Salt Lake City and decided to work for himself. He bought a run-down hotel in Portland and then brought Sato and her siblings back home. Now they were on their way to get her mother's piano from the lady who kept it for them.

The woman greeted her with a hug and then led her to a back room. There was mother's piano. The wood was warped and chipped away in some places. "I'm so sorry," said the woman, "but I only had room for it here near the heater. It's been through a lot."

Sato smiled. "So have we," she said.

Susumu Satow

A military hospital somewhere in France
October 17, 1944, 6:00 p.m.

Satow sat up in his hospital bed as the pretty nurse took his temperature. "Normal," she said, reading the thermometer. "How are you feeling today?"

"Better every day," replied Satow with a smile.

"Glad to hear it," said the nurse. "I'll stop by later and check in on you."

He had been wounded in the back from shrapnel while fighting the Germans in the Vosges Mountains of France. The 442nd had suffered devastating losses in the fierce fighting. Only he and two other men from his company had survived the battle. Before that, they had been stationed in Italy, north of Rome, fighting the Italians. Satow was grateful to be alive but was eager to be back in the fight. He felt he owed it to his comrades, those brave Nisei who had given their lives for their country.

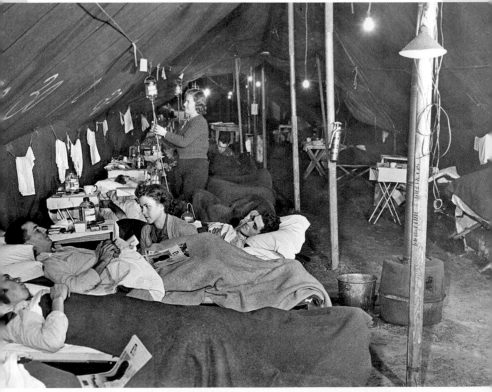

Many of the wounded in World War II were treated in field hospitals.

Harvey Itano

Detroit Receiving Hospital, Michigan
July 8, 1945, 1:15 p.m.

Harvey Itano was just getting used to people calling him Dr. Itano now that he had received his medical degree earlier that month. His parents, who made the trip to St. Louis, could not have been prouder of him. The war in Europe had ended in May with Germany and Italy's defeat and now the Japanese were fighting a losing war in the Pacific. It was only a matter of time before they also faced defeat. His family and nearly all the Japanese American internees had been released to go home. They picked up their lives where they left off as best they could. As for Itano, he enjoyed his internship at the hospital. However, he was finding his real passion was not treating patients. He wanted to pursue biomedical research. Itano also wanted to return to his home state to be closer to his parents. California had some bad memories for him, but more good ones.

The Detroit Receiving Hospital in Michigan as it looked in the 1940s.

Hiroshi Kashiwagi

Loomis, California
January 5, 1946, 10:45 a.m.

It was a bittersweet homecoming for Kashiwagi. He and other no-no boys were among the last internees to be freed, nearly four months after the war had ended. At Tule Lake, a lawyer had met with him and others concerning their renunciation of their citizenship. He agreed to represent them in a legal fight to regain their citizenship.

Kashiwagi had his family's love and support, but to many other Nisei and white people, he was an outcast. He didn't care. Tomorrow he would start a job as a farm laborer to make enough money to support himself. He was also thinking about going back to college. The one good thing to come out of his time at Tule Lake was his discovery of his creative side as both an actor and writer. He wanted to pursue that further and to get a college degree. He thought he had a good story to tell the world—the story of the internment camps.

Japanese Americans took part in the Italian campaign in Naples, Italy.

EPILOGUE

The Japanese American internment program has come to be remembered as one of the most shameful events in American history. Fear and prejudice overruled reason and fairness. Only 10 Americans by war's end were convicted of spying for the Japanese. Not one of them was a Japanese American. On the other hand, 33,000 Japanese

Americans served with honor in the U.S. military during and directly after World War II. Eight hundred of them died in action.

Many internees returned from the camps to find their homes and property taken over by other people or businesses, and their livelihoods gone. In July 1948 Congress passed the Evacuation Claims Act. This allowed internees to file claims for damages or property loss. Although the government distributed $31 million, the claimants on average got less than 10 cents per dollar lost. By then, the internment camps seemed to have been forgotten by everyone but the people who lived in them.

But recognition slowly began to come. President Gerald Ford rescinded Executive Order 9066 on February 19, 1976, exactly 34 years to the day it was signed into law. Then in 1978, John Tateishi, who was a child in the Manzanar camp, became National Redress Director of the Japanese American Citizens League (JACL). For 10 years Tateishi led the fight to win financial redress for internees. His hard work and that of other JACL members finally resulted in President Ronald

Reagan signing a law in 1988 that offered $20,000 to each surviving internee. The first check given out two years later in a ceremony in Washington, D.C., went to 107-year-old Reverend Mamoru Eto.

Isamu Noguchi, who died in 1988, did not live to see the financial redress. On his return to New York City in late 1942, Noguchi wrote of his camp experience, "I was free finally of causes and

Isamu Noguchi designed the Garden of Peace for UNESCO's headquarters in Paris.

disillusions with mutuality. I resolved henceforth to be an artist only." But his experience in the camp had definitely influenced Noguchi's art. A bitterness and sense of the absurd can be seen in such post-internment works as *This Tortured Earth* and *The World Is a Foxhole*. By the time of his death, Noguchi's reputation as one of the most distinguished American sculptors was secure.

Mine Okubo's career as an illustrator flourished after she arrived in New York to work at *Fortune* magazine. In 1946, she published a book of her experiences as an internee, *Citizen 13660*. It contained more than 200 of her pen and ink sketches of camp life. It was the first book to be published about the camps written by an internee. It is still in print. Okubo, who devoted her last years to painting, died in 2001, at age 88.

Harvey Itano returned to California to do graduate work at the California Institute of Technology. There he earned doctorates in chemistry and physics in 1950. He worked with leading biochemist Linus Pauling on the genetic disease sickle cell anemia. His groundbreaking

Harvey Itano (standing, second from right) was among 10 outstanding chemists honored by the American Chemical Society in 1954.

work on sickle cell earned him the Martin Luther King Jr. Medical Achievement Award in 1972. Itano became the first Japanese American elected to the National Academy of Science and died at age 89 on May 8, 2010 in La Jolla, California.

Bess Chin married a Chinese man and moved to Berkeley, California. She has taught quilting at a Japanese American nutrition center. She made a quilt with her class representing the camp experiences of fellow internees.

Hiroshi Kashiwagi entered the University of California at Los Angeles (UCLA) in 1950, earning a degree in Oriental Languages. The year before, he founded a theater group, the Nisei Experimental Group in Los Angeles, and wrote plays for the troupe. His drama *Laughter and Fake Teeth*, staged in 1954, is generally considered the first produced play to be set in a Japanese American internment camp. Kashiwagi's first book, *Swimming in the American: A Memoir and Selected Writings*, won the American Book Award in 2005. After a long legal battle, Kashiwagi finally regained his U.S. citizenship in 1959.

Hiroshi Kashiwagi looks back at several photos of himself in 1945.

Susumu Satow returned to Italy after recovering from his wounds and continued to fight until the war in Europe ended in May 1945. He returned home to live in Sacramento, California, and worked at McClellan Air Force Base. He became an active member of the Veterans of Foreign Wars (VFW) and served on the board of directors of the 100th-442nd Military Intelligence Service World War II Memorial Foundation. He helped plan and build the Poston Memorial Monument and Kiosk in Arizona to commemorate the Japanese Americans who were held there. In November 2011 Satow received the Congressional Gold Medal for his many years of service to his country. He died the following February at age 88.

Sato Hashizume became a nurse. She settled in San Francisco and taught nursing at the University of California branch there.

Marielle Tsukamoto attended the University of the Pacific and graduated with a BA in education. She taught school for 25 years and retired as a school administrator in 2001. She continues to educate the public about the internment camps

Marielle Tsukamoto made a career of educating people about history.

and is on the board of directors of the National Women's History Project.

John Tateishi continued to work for his fellow Japanese Americans. In 1999 he became National Executive Director of the Japanese American Citizens League (JACL), the oldest and largest Asian American civil rights organization in th United States. The same year he published *Justice for All*, an oral history of the intern camps. He served as JACL director unti

...s in the internment camps—and the people who were held in ... brought to vivid life by Dorothea Lange's photographs.

Dorothea Lange continued to be a leading American photographer until her death in 1965. Seven years later a selection of her internment camp photographs was finally shown publicly in a well-received traveling exhibition. One of the exhibit stops was a department store in Tokyo, Japan. These same photos were published in a book, *Executive Order 9066*, in 1972.

While most of the internees went on to have successful and productive lives after the camps, they carried the scars of that experience all their days. John Tateishi, returning to Manzanar in 1975 as an adult, wrote this about his visit: ". . . as I sat there looking at the fading light of Manzanar, [I thought] no one really ever leaves this place . . . somewhere on the desert of America, I'm still a young boy running in the wind."

Mine Okubo, in an interview near the end of her life, had this to say about the internment camps: "I hope that things can be learned from this tragic episode, for I believe it could happen again."

It is our responsibility as Americans to see that it doesn't.

TIMELINE

DECEMBER 7, 1941: The Japanese attack the U.S. naval base at Pearl Harbor in Hawaii, killing more than 2,000 service people and civilians, damaging six battleships and destroying two.

DECEMBER 8, 1941: The United States declares war on Japan and becomes a participant on the Allies' side in World War II.

FEBRUARY 19, 1942: President Franklin D. Roosevelt signs Executive Order 9066, authorizing the establishment of "military areas" that would exclude "any or all persons" the military felt needed to be excluded. Japanese Americans living on the West Coast are at the head of this list.

MARCH 21, 1942: The first Japanese American evacuees from Los Angeles arrive at the Manzanar War Relocation Reception Center in eastern California.

MARCH–JUNE 1942: Photographer Dorothea Lange, working for the War Relocation Authority (WRA), takes hundreds of pictures of Japanese American internees in several assembly centers and the Manzanar internment camp.

MAY 1, 1942: Artist Mine Okubo arrives at Tanforan Assembly Center with her brother, Toku.

MAY 8, 1942: Well-known sculptor Isamu Noguchi arrives at the Poston, Arizona, internment camp, hoping to start an ambitious art program for internees.

MAY–SEPTEMBER 1942: The majority of more than 110,000 Japanese Americans living on the West Coast are moved into nine relocation camps in six states.

OCTOBER 6, 1942: Jerome, Arkansas, the last relocation center, opens. It is one of only two camps in the United States east of the Rocky Mountains.

DECEMBER 6, 1942: An internee demonstration over the arrest of two residents leads to a riot in Manzanar. One resident is shot dead as guards respond to the riot.

FEBRUARY 1, 1943: President Roosevelt officially announces the formation of the 442nd Combat Team, the first all-Japanese American military unit.

FEBRUARY 1, 1943: The so-called "loyalty questionnaire" is given to all internees over 17 years of age, a tool for army recruitment and the segregation of "disloyal" internees.

JULY 15, 1943: Tule Lake is designated as an official segregation center for those who unsatisfactorily responded to the questionnaire, the so-called "no-no boys."

JANUARY 11, 1944: Mine Okubo leaves the Topaz, Utah, camp for New York City to work as an illustrator for *Fortune* magazine.

MAY 1944: The 442nd Regimental Combat Team, which Sus Satow is part of, is shipped off to Italy.

JULY 1945: Former Manzanar internee Harvey Itano receives his medical degree from St. Louis University's School of Medicine.

AUGUST 6, 1945: The United States drops an atomic bomb on the Japanese city of Hiroshima and three days later drops another bomb on Nagasaki.

SEPTEMBER 2, 1945: The Japanese officially surrender, ending World War II.

OCTOBER 15, 1945–DECEMBER 15, 1945: The WRA officially closes all internment camps, except for the Tule Lake Segregation Center.

MARCH 1946: Tule Lake officially closes and the last of the internees are released.

GLOSSARY

alien (AL-yuhn)—a foreign-born resident who has not become a naturalized citizen

barracks (BAR-uhks)—a group of buildings where people live, usually in a military context

black market (BLAK MAR-kit)—a place where goods are sold illegally, in violation of official rules

Caucasian (ko-KA-zhuhn)—a racial division of people whose ancestors came from Europe, parts of North Africa, India, and Western Asia

curfews (KUR-fyoorz)—official orders requiring persons to remain indoors during certain times, especially at night

defiled (di-FILD)—spoiled or tainted

immigrants (IM-uh-gruhnts)—people who move from their homeland to reside permanently in another country

internment camps (in-TURN-muhnt KAMPS)—places where a government confines certain people, often during a time of war

Issei (es-SA)—a Japanese person who immigrates to North America, especially before World War II

Kibei (KE-ba)—a person of Japanese descent born in North America but educated in Japan

mess hall (MES HOL)—a place where a group of people take meals together regularly

Nisei (NE-sa)—a person born in North America whose parents were immigrants from Japan

propaganda (PRAW-puh-GAN-duh)—information spread to try to influence the thinking of people; often not completely true or fair

public domain (PUB-lik do MAIN)—status of a work no longer protected by copyright

quarantine (KOWR-uhn-teen)—the isolation of people with a contagious disease to prevent it from spreading to others

redress (RE-dres)—setting right a moral wrong, often with financial compensation

Sansei (san-SA)—a person born in North America whose grandparents were immigrants from Japan, a third generation Japanese American

shrapnel (SHRAP-nahl)—fragments from an exploding shell

tuberculosis (too-bur-kyuh-LO-sis)—an infectious disease that especially affects the lungs

CRITICAL THINKING QUESTIONS

1. Some Germans and Italians, whose countries were also at war with the United States, were sent to internment camps. But the number was only a fraction of the number of Japanese Americans in camps. Also, these people were German or Italian nationals who happened to be in the United States when war broke out, not American citizens or aliens. Why do you think Japanese Americans were singled out for this punishment?

2. Only Japanese Americans living on the West Coast in the so-called "war zone" were forced to go to the internment camps. Why do you think that Japanese Americans in other parts of the country were not sent to these camps?

3. The Nisei, the Kibei, and the Issei were often at odds in the camps about how to respond to the injustices they endured. How do you think their outlooks were different and why? Use details from the book and your own thinking in your response.

INTERNET SITES

Japanese American Internment Facts for Kids
https://kids.kiddle.co/Japanese_American_internment

Japanese Internment Camps
www.historyforkids.net/japanese-internment-camps.html

World War II: Japanese Internment Camps
https://www.ducksters.com/history/world_war_ii/japanese_interment_camps.php

FURTHER READING

Fein, Eric. *Mystery at Manzanar: A World War II Internment Camp Story.* North Mankato, MN: Stone Arch Books, 2008.

Moss, Marissa, and Yuko Shimizu. *Barbed Wire Baseball: How One Man Brought Hope to the Japanese Internment Camps of World War II.* New York: Abrams Books for Young Readers, 2016.

Sandler, Martin W. *Imprisoned: The Betrayal of Japanese Americans During World War II.* New York: Walker Books for Young Readers, 2013.

Takei, George, Justin Eisinger, and Steven Scott. *They Called Us Enemy.* Marietta, GA: Top Shelf Productions, 2019.

SELECTED BIBLIOGRAPHY

Gordon, Linda. *Dorothea Lange: A Life Beyond Limits.* New York: Norton, 2009.

Gordon, Linda, and Gary Y. Okihiro, editors. *Impounded: Dorothea Lange and the Censored Images of Japanese-American Internment.* New York: Norton, 2006.

Harth, Erica, editor. *Last Witnesses: Reflections on the Wartime Internment of Japanese Americans.* New York: Palgrave, 2001.

Ng, Wendy. *Japanese American Internment During World War II: A History and Reference Guide.* Westport, CT: Greenwood Press, 2002.

Okubo, Mine. *Citizen 13660.* Seattle, Washington: University of Washington Press, 1994.

Reeves, Richard. *Infamy: The Shocking Story of the Japanese American Internment in World War II.* New York: Henry Holt, 2015.

"Telling Their Stories: Japanese Americans Interned During WWII," www.tellingstories.org/internment/ Accessed February 10, 2019.

Ward, Geoffrey C., and Ken Burns. *The War: An Intimate History 1941-1945.* New York: Alfred A. Knopf, 2007.

INDEX

ABOUT THE AUTHOR

Steven Otfinoski has written more than 200 books for young readers. His previous books in the Tangled History series include *Day of Infamy: Attack on Pearl Harbor* and *Smooth Seas and a Fighting Chance: The Story of the Sinking of Titanic*. Among his many other books for Capstone are the You Choose book *World War II Infantrymen* and *Split History of the Battle of Fort Sumter*. Three of his nonfiction books have been named Books for the Teen Age by the New York Public Library. He lives in Connecticut with his wife and dog.